Christmas Carols for
Ukulele

Arranged by John King

ISBN 978-1-4234-5651-3

HAL•LEONARD®
CORPORATION
7777 W. BLUEMOUND RD. P.O. BOX 13819 MILWAUKEE, WI 53213

In Australia Contact:
Hal Leonard Australia Pty. Ltd
4 Lentara Court
Cheltenham, Victoria, 3192 Australia
Email: ausadmin@halleonard.com.au

Visit Hal Leonard Online at
www.halleonard.com

4	Angels We Have Heard on High
6	Away in a Manger
8	Coventry Carol
10	Deck the Hall
12	The First Noël
14	Go, Tell It on the Mountain
16	God Rest Ye Merry, Gentlemen
18	Good King Wenceslas
20	Hark! The Herald Angels Sing
22	Here We Come A-Wassailing
7	I Heard the Bells on Christmas Day
24	It Came Upon the Midnight Clear
26	Jesu, Joy of Man's Desiring
28	Jingle Bells
25	Joy to the World
30	O Christmas Tree
31	O Come, All Ye Faithful (Adeste Fideles)
32	O Come, O Come Immanuel
34	O Holy Night
33	O Little Town of Bethlehem
36	Silent Night
37	Toyland
38	Up on the Housetop
40	We Three Kings of Orient Are
39	We Wish You a Merry Christmas
42	What Child Is This?

Angels We Have Heard on High

Traditional French Carol
Translated by James Chadwick

First note

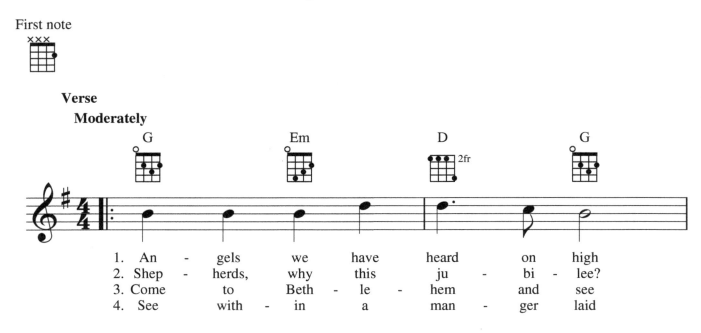

Verse

Moderately

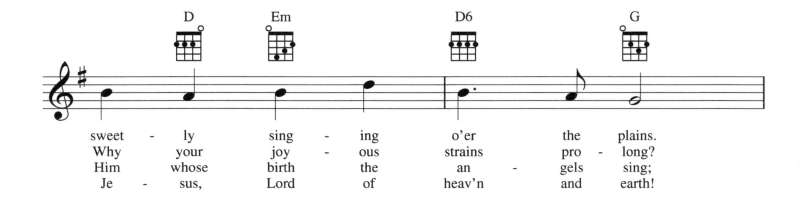

1. An - gels we have heard on high
2. Shep - herds, why this ju - bi - lee?
3. Come to Beth - le - hem and see
4. See with - in a man - ger laid

sweet - ly sing - ing o'er the plains.
Why your joy - ous strains pro - long?
Him whose birth the an - gels sing;
Je - sus, Lord of heav'n and earth!

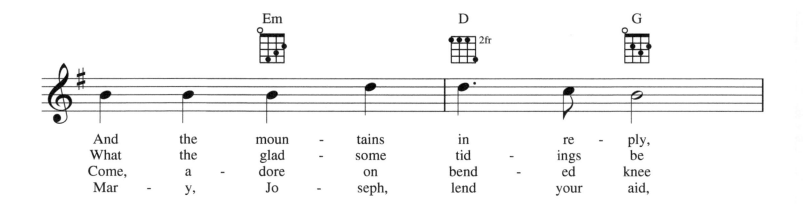

And the moun - tains in re - ply,
What the glad - some tid - ings be
Come, a - dore on bend - ed knee
Mar - y, Jo - seph, lend your aid,

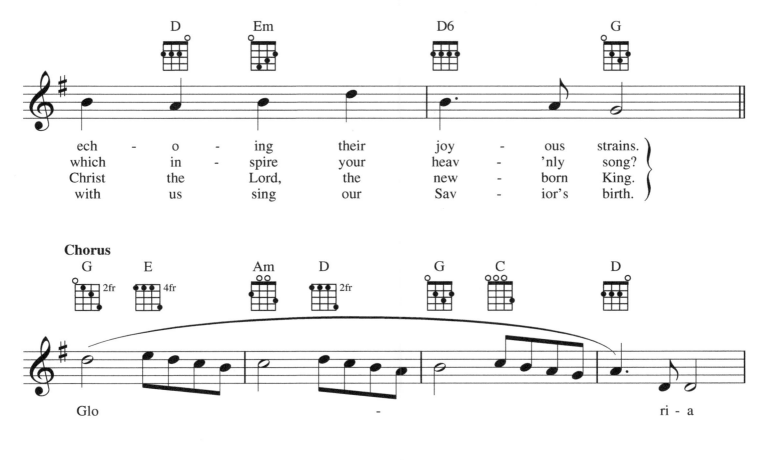

ech - o - ing their joy - ous strains.
which in - spire your heav - 'nly song?
Christ the Lord, the new - born King.
with us sing our Sav - ior's birth.

Chorus

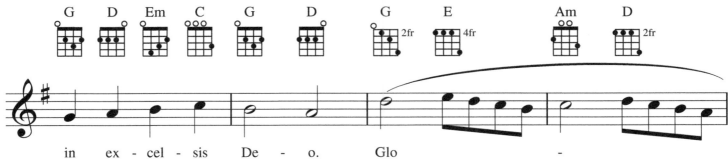

Glo - ri - a

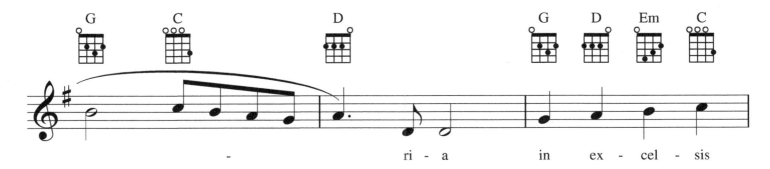

in ex - cel - sis De - o. Glo -

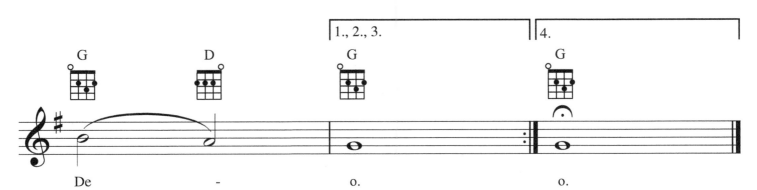

- ri - a in ex - cel - sis

De - o. o.

Away in a Manger

Words by John T. McFarland (V. 3)
Music by James R. Murray

I Heard the Bells on Christmas Day

Words by Henry Wadsworth Longfellow
Music by John Baptiste Calkin

Additional Lyrics

3. And in despair I bowed my head:
   "There is no peace on earth," I said,
   "For hate is strong, and mocks the song
   Of peace on earth, good will to men."

4. Then pealed the bells more loud and deep:
   "God is not dead, nor doth He sleep;
   The wrong shall fail, the right prevail,
   With peace on earth, good will to men."

5. Till, ringing, singing on its way,
   The world revolved from night to day,
   A voice, a chime, a chant sublime,
   Of peace on earth, good will to men!

Coventry Carol

Words by Robert Croo
Traditional English Melody

First note

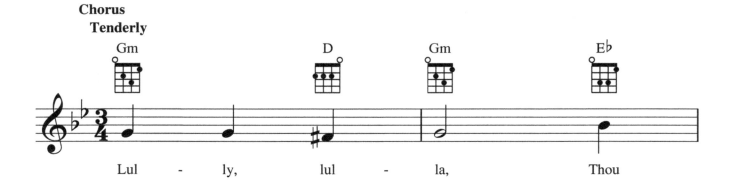

Chorus
Tenderly

| Gm | | D | Gm | Eb |

Lul - ly, lul - la, Thou

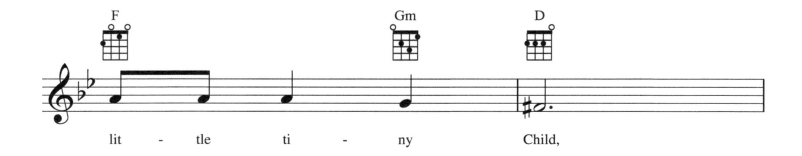

| F | | | Gm | D |

lit - tle ti - ny Child,

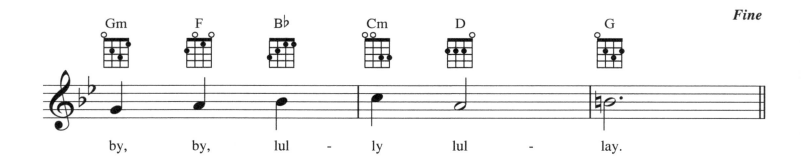

Fine

| Gm | F | Bb | Cm | D | G |

by, by, lul - ly lul - lay.

Verse

| Gm | D | Gm | Eb | F | Gm | D |

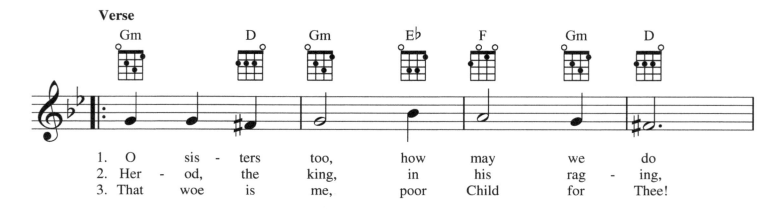

1. O sis - ters too, how may we do
2. Her - od, the king, in his rag - ing,
3. That woe is me, poor Child for Thee!

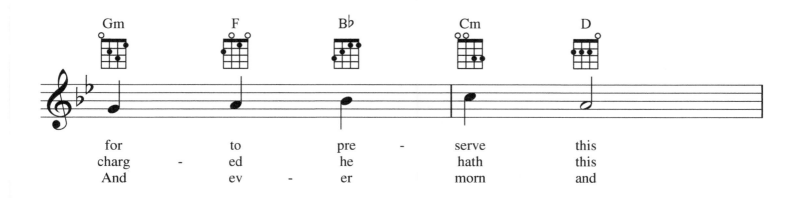

for   to   pre -   serve   this   this
charg -   ed   he   hath   morn   this
And   ev -   er   morn   this   and

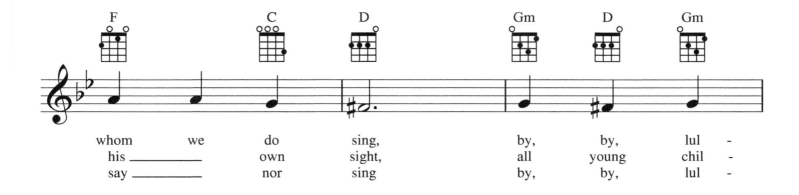

day   this   poor   Young - ling   for
day.   His   men   of   might,   in
day,   for   Thy   part - ing   nei -   ther

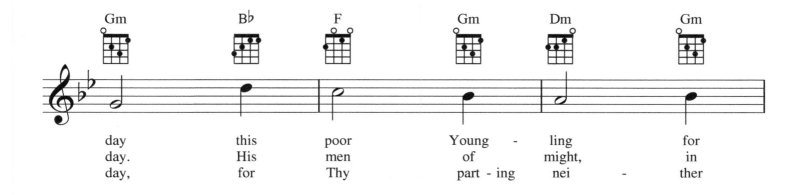

whom   we   do   sing,   by,   by,   lul -
his _____ own   sight,   all   young   chil -
say _____ nor   sing   by,   by,   lul -

1., 2.   *3.*   ***D.C. al Fine***

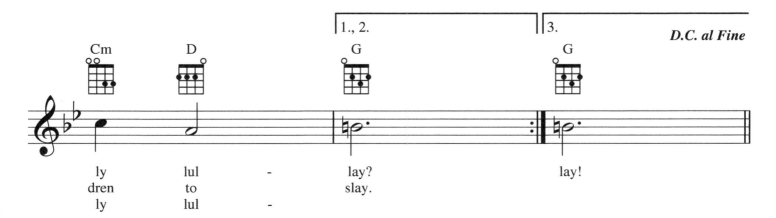

ly   lul -   lay?   lay!
dren   to   slay.
ly   lul -

Deck the Hall

Traditional Welsh Carol

First note

Verse
Lively

1. Deck the hall with boughs of hol - ly;
2. See the blaz - ing yule be - fore us;
3. Fast a - way the old year pas - ses;

fa, la, la, la, la, la, la, la, la.
fa, la, la, la, la, la, la, la, la.
fa, la, la, la, la, la, la, la, la.

'Tis the sea - son to be jol - ly;
Strike the harp and join the chor - us;
Hail the new ye lads and las - ses;

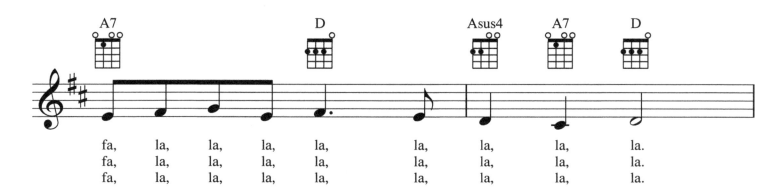

fa, la, la, la, la, la, la, la, la.
fa, la, la, la, la, la, la, la, la.
fa, la, la, la, la, la, la, la, la.

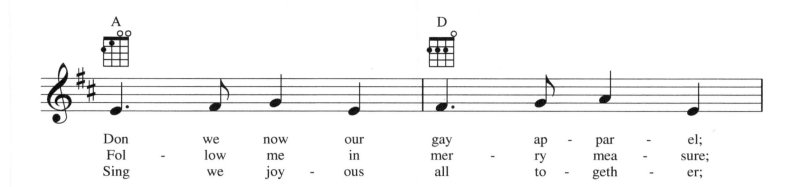

Don we now our gay ap - par - el;
Fol - low me in mer - ry mea - sure;
Sing we joy - ous all to - geth - er;

fa, la, la, la, la, la, la, la, la.
fa, la, la, la, la, la, la, la, la.
fa, la, la, la, la, la, la, la, la.

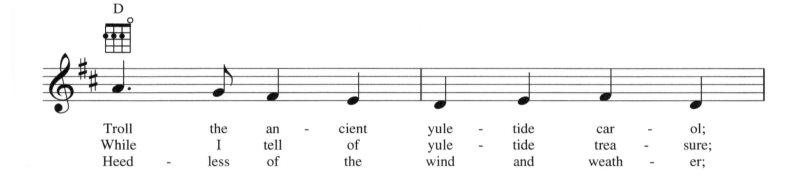

Troll the an - cient yule - tide car - ol;
While I tell of yule - tide trea - sure;
Heed - less of the wind and weath - er;

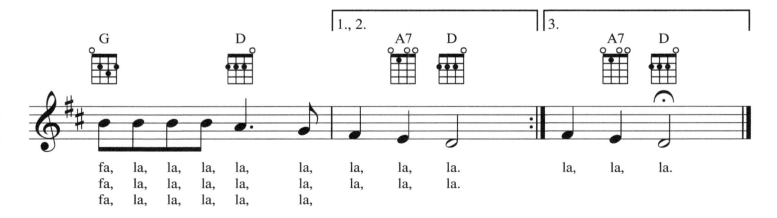

fa, la, la, la, la, la, la, la, la.   la, la, la.
fa, la, la, la, la, la, la, la, la.
fa, la, la, la, la, la,

The First Noël

17th Century English Carol
Music from W. Sandys' Christmas Carols

Chorus

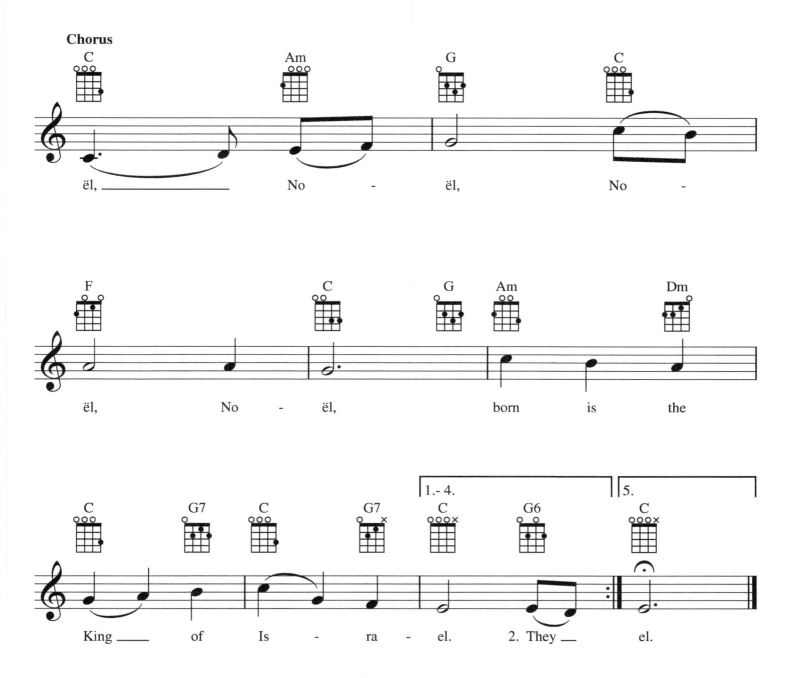

ël, _____ No - ël, No -

ël, No - ël, born is the

King _____ of Is - ra - el. 2. They ____ el.

Additional Lyrics

2. They looked up and saw a star
   Shining in the east, beyond them far.
   And to the earth it gave great light
   And so it continued both day and night.

3. And by the light of that same star,
   Three wise men came from country far;
   To seek for a King was their intent,
   And to follow the star wherever it went.

4. This star drew nigh to the northwest,
   O'er Bethlehem it took its rest;
   And there it did both stop and say,
   Right over the place where Jesus lay.

5. Then entered in those wise men three,
   Full reverently upon their knee;
   And offered there in His presence,
   Their gold, and myrrh, and frankincense.

Go, Tell It on the Mountain

African-American Spiritual
Verses by John W. Work, Jr.

First note

Chorus
Lively

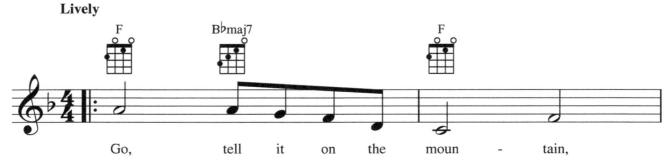

Go, tell it on the moun - tain,

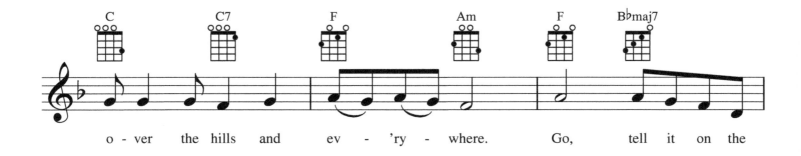

o - ver the hills and ev - 'ry - where. Go, tell it on the

To Coda ⊕   *Fine*

moun - tain that Je - sus Christ _ is born.

{ 1. While
{ 2. The
{ 3. Down

Verse

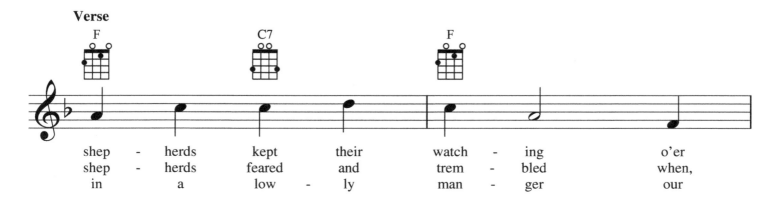

shep - herds kept their watch - ing o'er
shep - herds feared and trem - bled when,
in a low - ly man - ger our

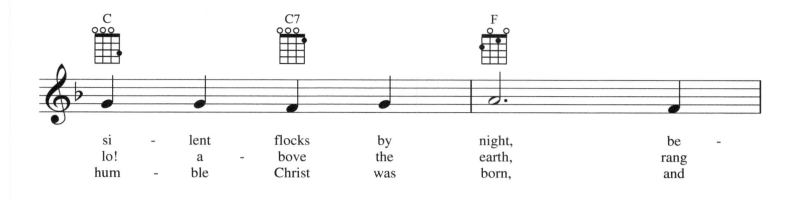

si - lent flocks by night, be -
lo! a - bove the earth, rang
hum - ble Christ was born, and

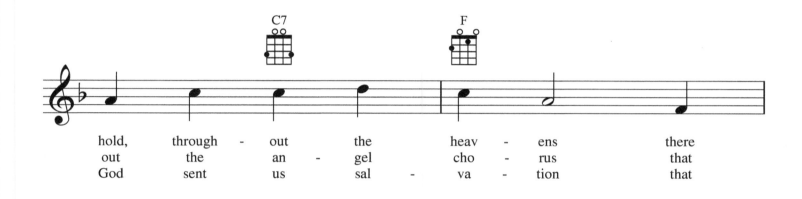

hold, through - out the heav - ens there
out the an - gel cho - rus that
God sent us sal - va - tion that

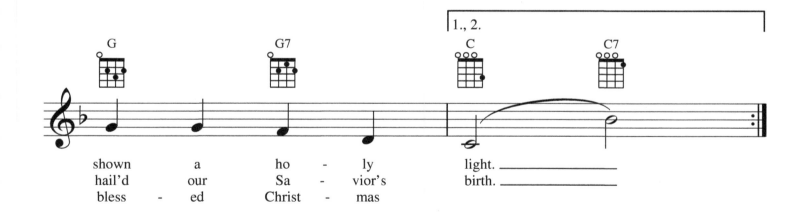

1., 2.

shown a ho - ly light. _____
hail'd our Sa - vior's birth. _____
bless - ed Christ - mas

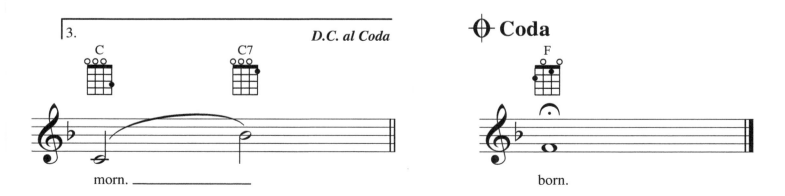

3.

D.C. al Coda

morn. _____

⊕ Coda

born.

God Rest Ye Merry, Gentlemen

19th Century English Carol

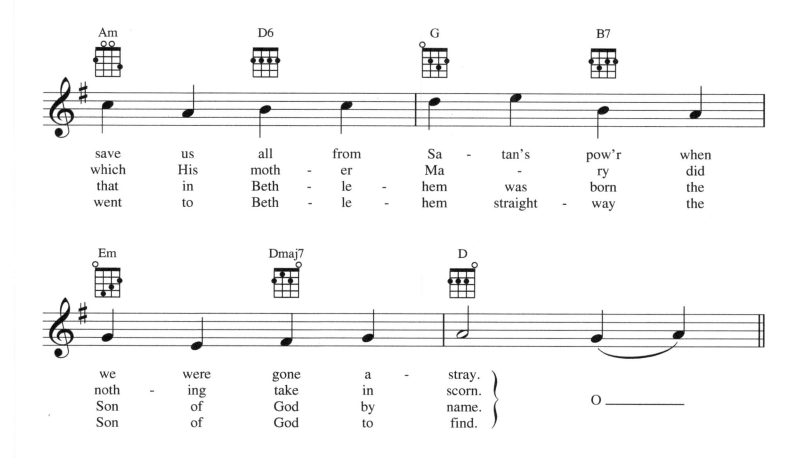

save us all from Sa - tan's pow'r when
which His moth - er Ma - ry did
that in Beth - le - hem was born the
went to Beth - le - hem straight - way the

we were gone a - stray.
noth - ing take in scorn.
Son of God by name.
Son of God to find.

O _____

Chorus

tid - ings of com - fort and joy, com - fort and

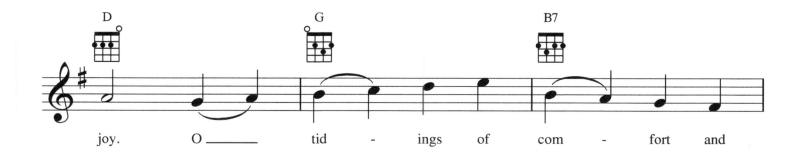

joy. O _____ tid - ings of com - fort and

1.-3. | 4.

joy. _____

2. In
3. From
4. Now

Good King Wenceslas

Words by John M. Neale
Music from Piae Cantiones

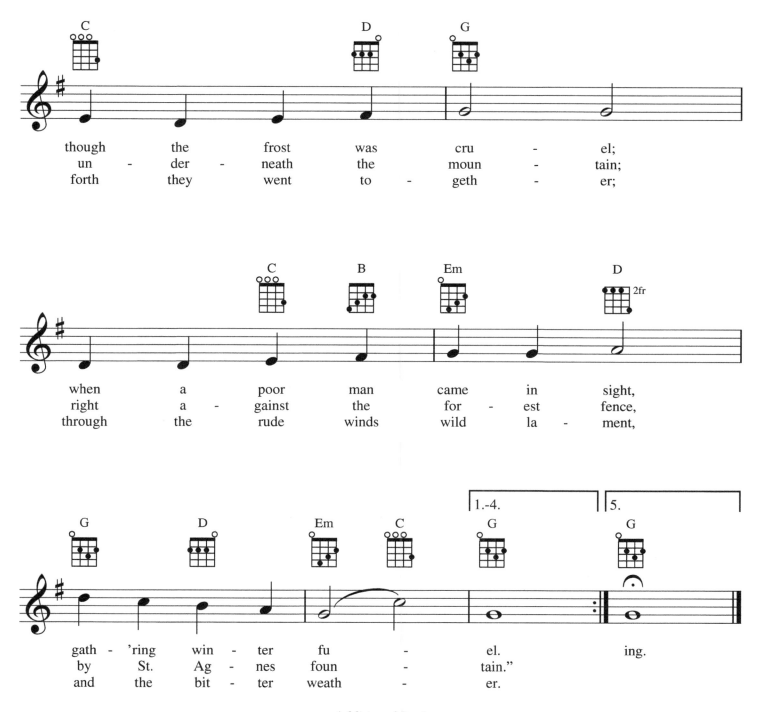

though the frost was cru - el;
un - der - neath the cru moun - tain;
forth they went to - geth - er;

when a poor man came in sight,
right a - gainst the for - est fence,
through the rude winds wild la - ment,

gath - 'ring win - ter fu - el.
by St. Ag - nes foun - tain."
and the bit - ter weath - er.

ing.

Additional Lyrics

4. "Sire, the night is darker now,
   And the wind blows stronger;
   Fails my heart, I know not how,
   I can go no longer."
   "Mark my footsteps, my good page,
   Tread thou in them boldly;
   Thou shalt find the winter's rage
   Freeze thy blood less coldy."

5. In his master's steps he trod,
   Where the snow lay dinted;
   Heat was in the very sod
   Which the saint has printed.
   Therefore, Christmas men, be sure,
   Wealth or rank possessing;
   Ye who now will bless the poor,
   Shall yourselves find blessing.

Hark! The Herald Angels Sing

Words by Charles Wesley
Altered by George Whitefield
Music by Felix Mendelssohn-Bartholdy
Arranged by William H. Cummings

Join the tri - umph of the skies. _____
Hail th'in - car - nate De - i - ty. _____
Born that man no more may die. _____

With th'an - gel - ic hosts pro - claim,
Pleased as man with man to dwell,
Born to raise the sons of earth,

"Christ is _____ born in Beth - le - hem."
Je - sus, _____ our Im - man - u - el.
born to _____ give them sec - ond birth.

Chorus

Hark! the her - ald an - gels sing,

1., 2.
3.

"Glo - ry _____ to the new-born King!" new-born King!"

Here We Come A-Wassailing

Traditional

First note

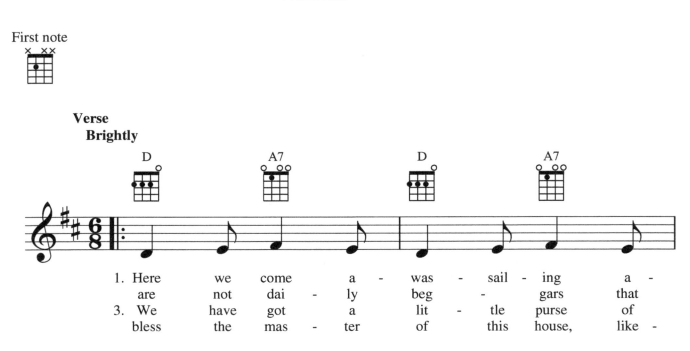

1. Here we come a - was - sail - ing a -
   are we not dai - ly beg - gars that
3. We have got a lit - tle purse of
   bless the mas - ter of this house, like -

mong the leaves so green.
beg from door to door, _____ but
stretch - ing leath - er skin; _____ we
wise the mis - tress too; _____ and

Here we come a - wand' - ring, so fair _____ to be
we are neigh - bor chil - dren whom you have seen be -
want a lit - tle mon - ey to line the well with -
all the lit - tle chil - dren that round the ta - ble

Chorus

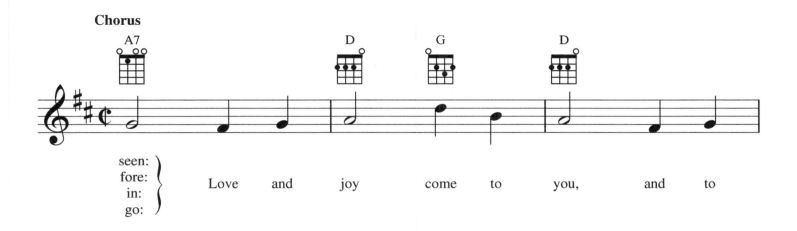

seen:
fore:
in:
go:

Love and joy come to you, and to

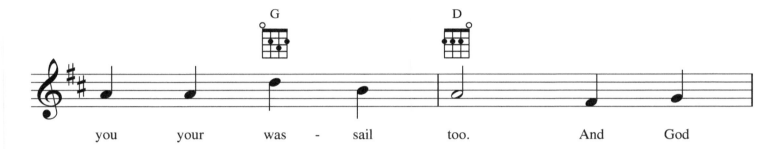

you your was - sail too. And God

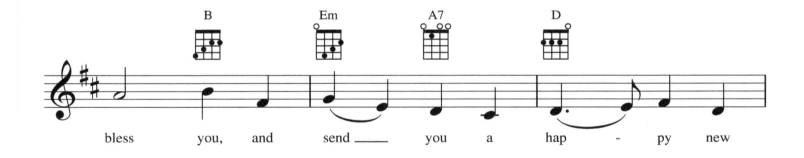

bless you, and send ____ you a hap - py new

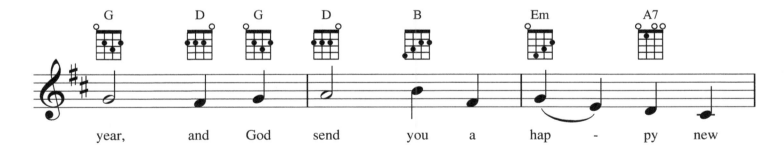

year, and God send you a hap - py new

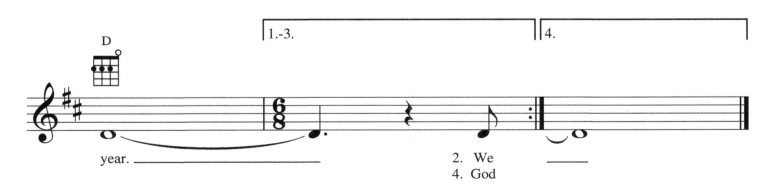

1.-3.   4.

year. ____   2. We ____
                    4. God

It Came Upon the Midnight Clear

Words by Edmund Hamilton Sears
Music by Richard Storrs Willis

Joy to the World

Words by Isaac Watts
Music by George Frideric Handel
Adapted by Lowell Mason

Jesu, Joy of Man's Desiring

English Words by Robert Bridges
Music by Johann Sebastian Bach

First note

Verse
Moderately

1. Je - su, joy of man's de - sir - ing,
2. Through the way where hope is guid - ing,

ho - ly wis - dom, love ___ most ___ bright.
hark, what peace - ful mu - sic ___ rings!

Drawn by Thee, our souls as - pir - ing,
Where the flock in Thee con - fid - ing,

soar to un - cre - at - ed ___ light.
drink of joy from death - less ___ springs.

Word of God, our flesh _____ that fash - ioned,
Theirs is beau - ty's fair - est plea - sure,

with the fire of life _____ im - pas - sioned.
theirs is wis - dom's ho - liest trea - sure.

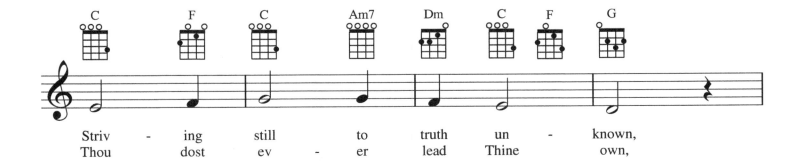

Striv - ing still to truth un - known,
Thou dost still ev - er truth lead Thine own,

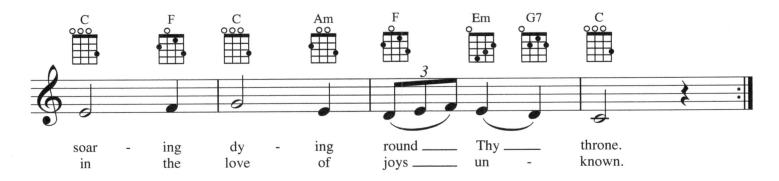

soar - ing dy - ing round _____ Thy _____ throne.
in the dy love of joys _____ un - known.

Jingle Bells

Words and Music by J. Pierpont

O Christmas Tree

Traditional German Carol

O Come, All Ye Faithful

(Adeste Fidelis)

Music by John Francis Wade
Latin Words translated by Frederick Oakeley

O Come, O Come Immanuel

Plainsong, 13th Century
Words translated by John M. Neale and Henry S. Coffin

O Little Town of Bethlehem

Words by Phillips Brooks
Music by Lewis H. Redner

First note

Verse
Slowly

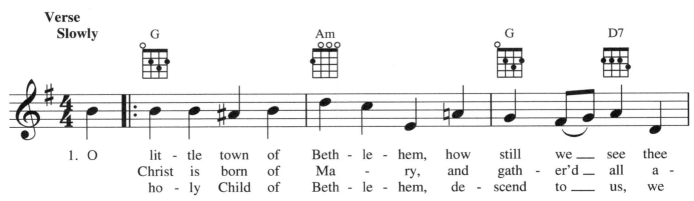

1. O lit - tle town of Beth - le - hem, how still we __ see thee
Christ is born of Ma - ry, and gath - er'd __ all a -
ho - ly Child of Beth - le - hem, de - scend to __ us, we

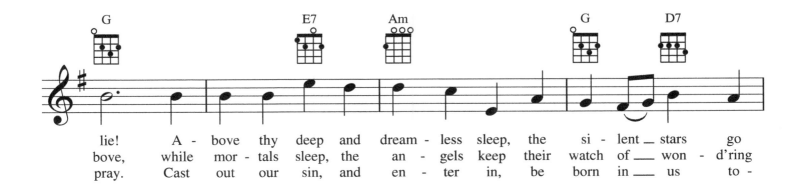

lie! A - bove thy deep and dream - less sleep, the si - lent __ stars go
bove, while mor - tals sleep, the an - gels keep their watch of __ won - d'ring
pray. Cast out our sin, and en - ter in, be born in __ us to -

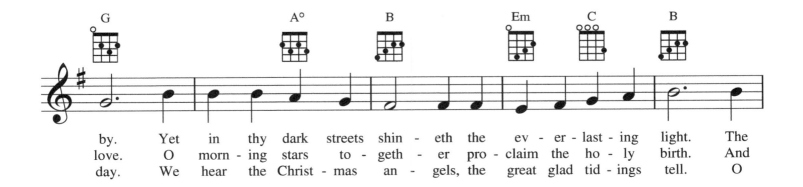

by. Yet in thy dark streets shin - eth the ev - er - last - ing light. The
love. O morn - ing stars to - geth - er pro - claim the ho - ly birth. And
day. We hear the Christ - mas an - gels, the great glad tid - ings tell. O

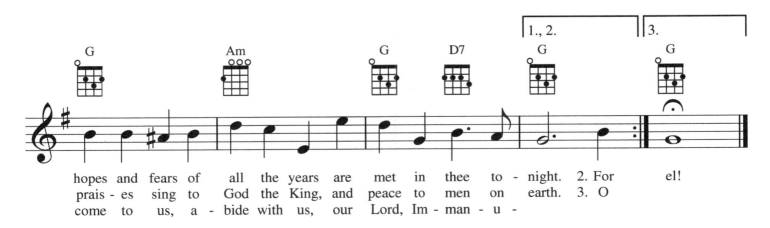

hopes and fears of all the years are met in thee to - night. 2. For el!
prais - es sing to God the King, and peace to men on earth. 3. O
come to us, a - bide with us, our Lord, Im - man - u -

O Holy Night

French Words by Placide Cappeau
English Words by John S. Dwight
Music by Adolphe Adam

34

Silent Night

Words by Joseph Mohr
Translated by John F. Young
Music by Franz X. Gruber

Toyland

from BABES IN TOYLAND

Words by Glen MacDonough
Music by Victor Herbert

Up on the Housetop

Words and Music by B. R. Hanby

1. Up on the house-top rein-deer pause, out jumps good old
2. First comes the stock-ing of lit-tle Nell. Oh, dear San-ta
3. Next comes the stock-ing of lit-tle Will. Oh, just see what a

San - ta Claus. Down through the chim - ney with lots of toys.
fill it well. Give her a dol - ly that laughs and cries,
glo - rious fill! Here is a ham - mer and lots of tacks,

Chorus

All for the lit - tle ones, Christ - mas joys.
one that will o - pen and shut her eyes. } Ho, ho, ho, who would - n't go?
al - so a ball and a whip that cracks.

Ho, ho, ho, who would - n't go? ___ Up on the house - top,

click, click, click. Down through the chim - ney with good Saint Nick. good Saint Nick.

We Wish You a Merry Christmas

Traditional English Folksong

We Three Kings of Orient Are

Words and Music by John H. Hopkins, Jr.

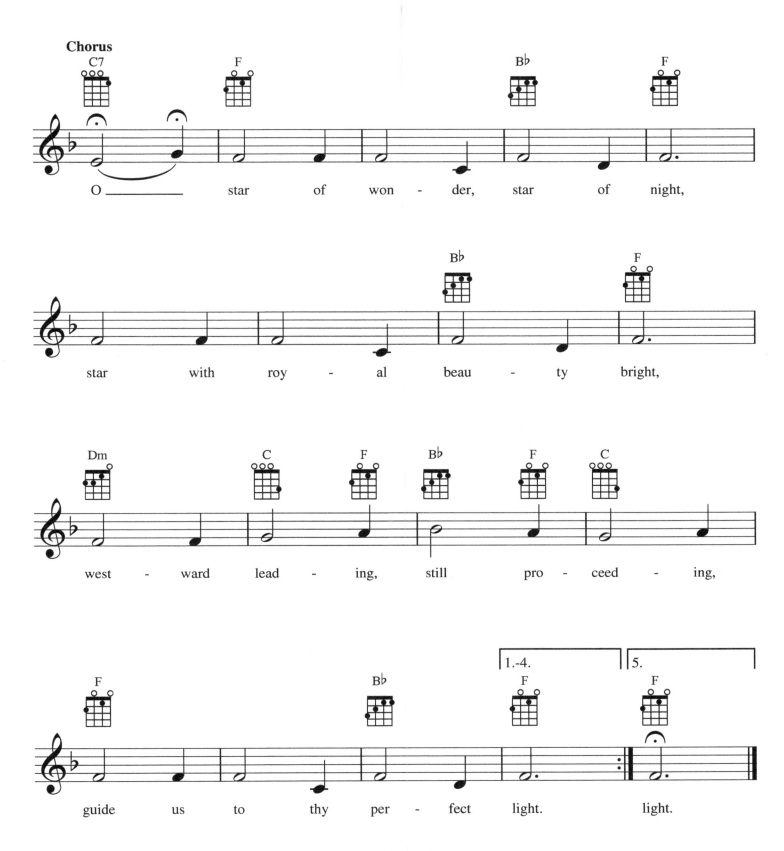

Additional Lyrics

4. Myrrh is mine; its bitter perfume
   Breathes a life of gathering gloom;
   Sorr'wing, sighing, bleeding, dying,
   Sealed in the stone-cold tomb.

5. Glorious now, behold Him arise,
   King and God and sacrifice.
   Alleluia, alleluia,
   Sounds through the earth and skies.

What Child Is This?

Words by William C. Dix
16th Century English Melody

Chorus

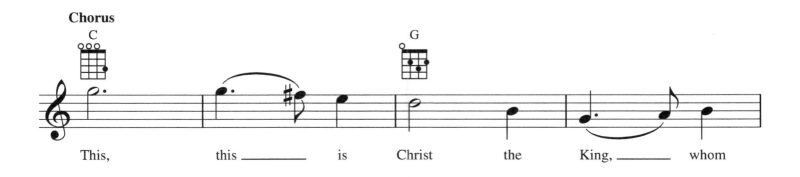

This, this ____ is Christ the King, ____ whom

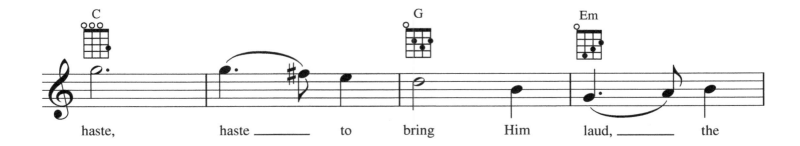

shep - herds guard ____ and an - gels sing;

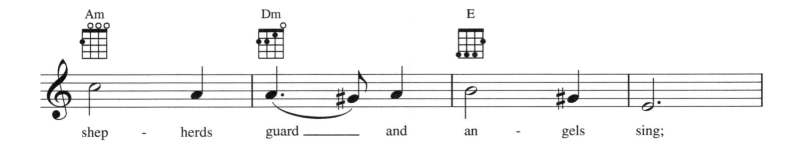

haste, haste ____ to bring Him laud, ____ the

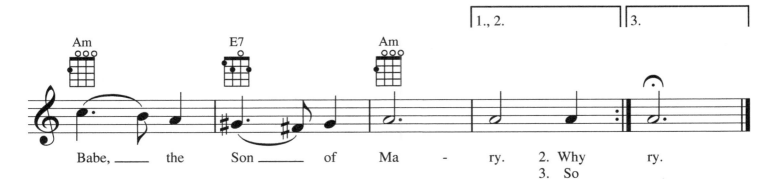

Babe, ____ the Son ____ of Ma - ry. 2. Why ry.
3. So